NATUROGRAPHY:
EXERCISES TO WAKEN OUR SENSES AND RECONNECT US TO NATURE

ERIN WATERMAN

DEDICATION

Our Home

CONTENTS

ACKNOWLEDGMENTS

These 20 exercises were created by me but informed by my experiences with nature connection via Project NatureConnect (http://ecopsych.com). Many thanks to my daughter Carli who developed the Dream Boat activity and supplied several photos. May the next generation of nature connectors flourish.

INTRODUCTION

NATUROGRAPHY

Exercises to waken our senses and reconnect us to the natural world's restorative feedback loop.

Naturography uses Nature + Writing, activating our old sensory brain in the natural world and validating that wisdom through our newer brain and language center.

If you are indoors or unable to access a natural area like a park, you can practice many of these exercises with houseplants, a pet, a fish tank or what you see out a window. Many of us spend over 95% of our lifetime indoors, so we can benefit from conscious steps to connect to nature.

TOOL KIT YOU MAY WANT TO CARRY:
Coloring implements (crayons, markers, pens etc.), small note
pad, optional camera and water bottle.

WHY GO TOWARD A NATURAL ATTRACTION?
Natural attraction ecology teaches that all Nature works through
an endless dance of natural attractions (water/thirst, bee/flower,
sunlight/life, on and on indefinitely). As we start to focus on and
move toward our own natural attractions, we soon recognize
what is uniquely safe, providing good feelings, and restorative
for us. In nature reconnection work, it is essential to always
follow your own attractions and if the connection should become
less attractive or lose its pull, move to another space that calls to
you.

Reflection Questions:
How does learning to follow your own attractions impact your
sense of yourself? What happens when you move on from areas
that feel unsafe or uncomfortable and make another choice?

WHY SEEK PERMISSION FROM NATURAL ATTRACTIONS?

Asking permission for assistance from a natural attraction I have found enhances my experience of whatever connection I am making. Consider a time you drove, cycled, walked or ran somewhere and you arrived at your destination without being able to recall a single thing you experienced along the journey. Now consider a time you observed all around you and felt aware of birdsong, wind, color, light, good feelings, and your own movement through space. Everything seemed to be speaking and connecting specifically to you. When we seek permission, we in essence say to ourselves and the surroundings "I am open to learning from you, I am equal to you, I mean you no harm."

Reflection Questions:
How does requesting consent from the world around you affect your self-trust? Can you think of ways we unconsciously approach nature as a resource to be used rather than a living, breathing extension of ourselves? How would you like to consciously remember your wisdom roots in Nature?

Each of the following 20 nature connection activities begins with the same first two steps, so they will not be repeated on each activity. Any of these activities can be done in a group with sharing as a final step.

Step 1: Go to an area you find attractive in nature. Make sure this area remains attractive to you after about 60 seconds. If it does not, move toward another area that holds attraction.

Step 2: Silently ask permission from this area to help you with your activity.

11

2 X 2 SCAVENGER HUNT

- Mark or visualize a boundary of 2 x 2 square feet using sticks, stones, leaves, anything natural. Your hunt area will include all the soil below you and everything above you to the thin blue line of space.
- Find and write down as many things on the Scavenger List as possible in 10 minutes.
- If in a group, share with the group what you would like, including how doing the activity made you feel. Did it validate your sense of self?

SCAVENGER LIST

Something heart shaped
Something living
Something mineral
Something in motion
Something soft
Something sharp
Something that represents a current challenge
Something that represents a current joy
A root
Something you want to learn more about
Something blue
Something green
Something red
Add your own to the list!

LISTENING TO NATURE

▨ Get comfortable in a safe area. For 3 minutes close your eyes and listen to every sound you can hear, inside or outside of you.

▨ After 3 minutes, open your eyes and write down as many items you heard as you can.

▨ Now take crayons/coloring tools, even a stick in sand, and draw an image of the sounds you experienced.

▨ If in a group, share your drawing and/or list, including how blocking out your visual sense made you feel.

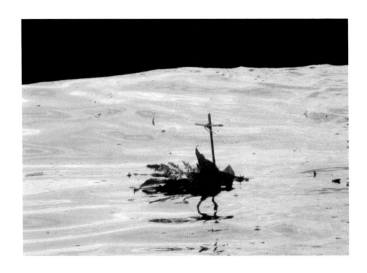

DREAM BOAT

- Go to an area with water: A river, stream, lake, ocean, pond, puddle. If you are limited to a sink or bathtub, go outside to collect nature's boat building items and bring them inside to float.
- Build a boat using only nature's gifts you find around you.
- Write down a dream you have. Place something that represents the dream or speak a dream you have for your life to the boat and let it float on the water. Do not worry if your boat is not seaworthy. Building it is the fun part. Your dream will be heard.
- Another variation you can try is to write down any worries or difficult feelings you have and place them in the boat to float instead of a dream you want to come true.

SMELL YOUR WAY TO SUCCESS

- This activity is best done in pairs, but can be done solo.
- Collect 5 items from your area (twig, stone, leaf, flower, etc).
- Smell each item one at a time until you feel confident you can tell them apart.
- Number them by placing a mark with a pencil or arranging them in a row.
- Close or blindfold your eyes. Have your activity partner hold one item up at a time out of sequence in front of your nose and try to identify it with only your sense of smell.
- Write down how using only your sense of smell made you feel. Were you successful? Did it validate you as a sensory being?
- Switch partners and repeat the steps.

19

SENSE A TREE

- Find a tree attractive to you.
- Touch as many parts of the tree as you can (root, trunk, branch, leaf). Close your eyes if you wish.
- Write down what you notice. Did it feel as you expected when you first approached it?
- Listen to any sounds the tree makes in wind. Write down what you notice.
- Smell the trunk. Does it remind you of anything? Write down what you notice.
- Reflect on and write down ways the tree benefits you, sharing its oxygen with your lungs, absorbing toxins and carbon dioxide from air, providing shade from sun, etc.
- If you wish, be the tree. Study how it stands and use your sense of body in space to become the tree.
- If you wish, create a sensory tree poem using the words you wrote down.
- If you wish, research your tree online using a free tree identifier to learn more about its place in the web.

ASK A QUESTION

- Sit for 10 minutes in your attraction area and ask an open-ended question you would like an answer to (not a yes/no question).
- Listen. Wait for an answer. Take as long as you wish.
- Record any animals or plants that visited your question and answer time.
- What did you learn about yourself?
- Write down what wisdom from your place in the natural world you have remembered by doing this activity.

23

COUNT BIRDS

- Find as many different birds as you can in 10 minutes, either visually or by sound. You do not need to learn their names to make a connection, but if you want to identify them using a bird guide you can. The goal is to count as many different ones as possible in your attractive area.
- What features stood out to you?
- Did they communicate with each other?
- With you?
- Write down everything you notice about the birds.

BE A COMPASS

 Make a circle around you using anything you find in your natural attraction area.

 Try to mark cardinal directions with your body. For example, stand and twist your torso with one arm stretched in front of you, one arm straight behind you while your feet are shoulder width apart.

 Write down how you figured out which direction is which (without consulting any device).

 How does this affect your trust in yourself?

 Make a mandala with the cardinal directions (East, West, North, South) using twigs, leaves, flower petals, grass, stones, etc., for decoration within the circle of the compass. Take a photo or simply admire and leave the work of art for others to admire and be recycled into Earth.

CLOUDSPOT

- Find an area where you can watch a cloud formation that catches your interest.
- Draw its shape.
- Does it remind you of anything familiar?
- Create a doodle from the shape.
- Do you know if the cloud is a signal of weather phenomena?
- Imagine a time before GPS, radar, Doppler weather maps. What might clouds tell you?
- If a cloud was a poem, what would it say?
- If in a group, share your cloud findings.

PLAY IN MUD

- Find a patch of mud or make some by mixing water with soil.
- Immerse your hands and/or feet in the mud.
- Look at your hand and/or foot prints.
- Make a mud cake or pie and decorate it like a professional baker would, except use items in nature found near you.
- The root of the word "human" is "hum" and "humus" or earth/ground, which became "humble" which finally became "human" from Latin "humanus."
- (After rinsing or brushing mud off) write down what you learned about yourself doing this activity. Was it difficult for you to embrace mud? Do you feel connected to earth?
- A recent study out of the United Kingdom published in the journal *Neuroscience* suggests there are friendly bacteria in soil that cause a reaction in the brain similar to antidepressants. So playing in mud might just make you happy!

SUNSET ENTERTAINMENT

- Sunsets seem to happen when most people are indoors watching TV or screens, but you can join the sunset entertainment revolution.
- Observe a sunset for 30 minutes preferably outside but through a window works as well. If you are unable to get to a spot where you can see much sky, record what you CAN see.
- Write down or photograph the sunset's colors or features that stood out to you. Watch three consecutive sunsets and record your findings.
- How were the sunsets different from one another?
- Did you notice any animal behavior at sunset?
- Do you prefer to go to sleep with the sun or stay awake late in an artificial light space?
- Did you sleep better than usual on the nights you watched a sunset?

BIG SKY

- Lie on your back on the ground somewhere you feel safe.
- Watch the sky, the clouds, and insect freeways during day or moon and stars at night.
- With modernization, there are fewer and fewer dark spaces for star viewing, but some states and national parks are creating dark parks internationally.
- Observe your patch of sky for at least 10 minutes on three separate occasions and write down your observations.
- Do you feel connected to the earth when doing this activity or connected to the big sky? Both?

EASY BEING GREEN

- In your chosen area, seek out and write down as many green things as you can.
- How many different shades of green can you identify?
- What was the first color you remember experiencing or learning as a child?
- What role does color in general play in human survival? Would you consider eating a food that naturally occurs in one color but appears another?
- What does green mean to you? Phrases exist like "green technology," "greening the Earth," "Green" political party, "green with envy," but what do you feel when you contemplate green?

NATURE'S GEOMETRY

- Find as many different shapes in your natural surroundings as you can.
- Draw at least 5.
- What patterns do you see?
- Can you find a flower or leaf that does not follow an expected pattern? (A four-leaf clover is one example). Why do you think this happens?
- What role does pattern have in your experience?
- If something violates a pattern, how does it make you feel?

NATURE'S DESIGN

- In observing your natural attraction area focus on one thing that makes you curious about how it functions.
- Write a list of questions you have about this one thing.
- Biomimicry is an entire field of engineering that mimics nature's design to develop products humans use. If you were a biomimicry engineer what one product would you like to design?
- What problem does your product solve for humans?
- What purpose do you think your chosen item to mimic serves in nature?

COLOR WHEEL

 Identify and write down as many colors as you can in your natural area in 10 minutes, below, around, above, and even from you (skin, eyes, etc.).

 Do you see some colors represented more than others?

 If so, why do you think this is? If not, why do you think so many colors exist in nature?

 Draw or paint anything using the colors from nature you identified in this exercise.

 How does this exercise make you feel about yourself?

Photo credit: Carli

INSECT FREEWAYS

- Focus on insects (arachnids/spiders are okay too) in your surroundings. Remember butterflies are insects too.
- How many different ones can you identify? There are about 200 million insects for every human, so your chances are better than good for finding some.
- Gently observe as many as you can and watch what they do. Would you have noticed them unless you were doing this focused activity?
- Write down how many modes of transportation you witness.
- Why do you think there are so many insects?
- What purposes do they serve in the web of life?
- If you have a fear of insects, what purpose does this fear serve?
- If you do have a lot of fear, take some time to research which insects are in your region and see if any of the ones you noted doing this activity are harmful to humans. You might be reassured.

Photo Credit: Carli

Photo Credit: Carli

WORM GRATITUDE

- Seek out a place with visible soil.
- Dig gently into the soil and see if you can find a worm or many. Do not harm the worms but simply observe them.
- If you have healthy soil, you likely have worms to thank. Worms help prevent soil erosion, break up hard soils, aerate soil during winters, help plants absorb more water, leave natural fertilizing compounds, minerals and bacteria to benefit plants, and per the Natural Resources Conservation Office, a single earthworm can digest 36 tons of soil in a year!
- Should you wish to take your worm gratitude to another level, there are countless resources for inexpensive DIY worm bins to help you turn your plant food waste into healthier soil for your garden.

"The soil is the great connector of lives, the source and destination of all. It is the healer and restorer and resurrector, by which disease passes into health, age into youth, death into life. Without proper care for it we can have no community, because without proper care for it we can have no life."
  - Wendell Berry

WEBSTRINGS

- Imagine invisible sensory lines connecting you to any one thing you focus on in nature.
- Practice identifying them and writing down any senses you feel activated between you and what you find attractive. Heat waves, coolness, vapor, light, trust, movement, color, sound, emotions.
- If you wish, draw a picture of these strings.
- Can you identify where the webstrings end?
- Are there strings between you and everything around you?
- Is there a break in the web of life?

INNER YOU/OUTER YOU

- Consider and write down a feeling that has been coming up for you this week.
- Consider and write down a challenge you are facing right now.
- Consider and write down something you find healing right now.
- Consider and write down something you are grieving right now.
- Consider and write down something that makes you laugh.
- Identify things in your natural attraction area you are drawn to. Figure out which five items mirror your above inner experiences and write these down.
- If possible, collect these items and arrange them into a creation you find beautiful.
- Take a photo or try to draw what you created.
- If in a group, share your creation with or without describing the meaning the natural items hold for you.

Photo Credit: Carli

BIBLIOGRAPHY

Berry, Wendell. (1996). *The Unsettling of America: Culture & Agriculture.* Sierra Club Books.

Biomimicry 3.8 is a leading resource for those interested in biomimicry (http://biomimicry.net/).

Cloud Appreciation Society published a handbook that helps you identify different cloud formations (http://cloudappreciationsociety.org/collectors-handbook/).

Cohen, Michael J. (2007). *Reconnecting With Nature, 3rd Ed.* Ecopress, An Imprint of Finney Company.

Lowry, C.A., Hollisa, J.H., de Vriesa, A., Pana, B., Brunetb, L.R., Huntb, J.R.F., Patonc, J.F.R., van Kampena, E., Knighta, D.M., Evansa, A.K., Rookb, G.A.W. & Lightmana, S.L. Identification of an immune-responsive mesolimbocortical serotonergic system: Potential role in regulation of emotional behavior. *Neuroscience* Available online 28 March 2007. doi:10.1016/j.neuroscience.2007.01.067

Natural Resources Conservation Service is a great resource for soil information (http://nrcs.usda.gov/wps/portal/nrcs/detailfull/soils/health/biology/).

Worm bin information can be found through this great source (http://www.bugabay.com).

Photo Credit: Carli

ABOUT THE AUTHOR

Erin Waterman spends every minute she can connecting to the natural world and dreaming of ways to encourage that connection as a healing source for others. You can find her at www.healingoutdoors.org.

Made in the USA
Monee, IL
13 October 2020